HOW TO CUT
Your
BUSINESS
COSTS

GW00701806

HOW TO CUT
Your
BUSINESS
COSTS

Peter D Brunt

KOGAN
PAGE

First published in Great Britain in 1988 by
Kogan Page Limited, 120 Pentonville Road,
London N1 9JN

British Library Cataloguing in Publication Data

Brunt, Peter D. (Peter Duncan)
    How to cut your business costs.
    1. Business firms. Financial management
    I. Title
    658.1'5

    ISBN 1-85091-671-3
    ISBN 1-85091-672-1 Pbk

Typeset by The Castlefield Press of Wellingborough
Printed and bound in Great Britain by
Biddles Ltd, Guildford

Contents

Introduction

An everyday challenge to business people and entrepreneurs is to find new ways and means of improving the profitability of their companies. Improved sales and margins are an obvious goal but a reduction in operating costs can often be easier and immediately beneficial. Remember that a reduction in cost is probably up to eight or ten times the value of an order received.

Many business managers do not have time constantly to check that every aspect of their business is being operated efficiently and cost-effectively. Employees perhaps do not have the automatic consciousness of the need to make profit by saving money. Consequently, as time goes by, practices within a company tend to lack the discipline that results in significant cost reduction.

Every business needs to look carefully at every item of expenditure to see if there are ways and means of reducing its costs.

Use this book to help to create an environment of cost-consciousness throughout the company. Perhaps a small committee could be organised which would co-opt the relevant people from time to time and meet with the intention of finding savings.

The book contains a comprehensive spread of topics including manufacturing, selling, distribution, finance and administration cost reduction. The ideas are intended to:

bring you new ideas for saving money;
encourage management to adapt these ideas to your circumstances;
act as a comprehensive cost reduction checklist;
provide a disciplined programme of action for achieving

7

significant cost reduction targets;
create a general cost-conscious environment.

The suggestions have been researched and compiled with the emphasis on practicability. Tick the boxes when you have implemented each proposal. If legal advice or other expert assistance is required, the services of a competent professional person should be sought.

Chapter 1

Credit Control, Cash Collection and Payment Terms

Most orders are fought for and won in a fiercely competitive market (and a great deal of expense is often incurred in the process) but snags, hold-ups and delays in getting paid often erode those treasured profit margins. In extreme instances a bad debt can turn a job into a loss, so no order can be considered complete until it has been paid for in full.

Giving credit beyond the agreed period costs money in terms of finance charges and administration. Take a look at the general payment picture and calculate the saving you would enjoy if debt collection were speeded up by an average of, say, seven days. Furthermore, list slow payers and see how many queries are holding up payment.

Your business may be well run and so may your client's, but business failures have a knack of hurting you from afar. So perhaps there is room in your company for saving and making money by reviewing your payment terms and tightening up still further on your credit control and cash collection procedures.

1. Review payment terms □

Settlement discounts should attract prompt payment. They could vary according to interest rate levels to provide the necessary incentive, but make sure that cash discounts are adjusted when interest rates fall. Also take a look at what your competitors allow.

2. Disallow cash discounts when payment is received late □

Most firms allow a few days over the due payment date. However, customers become aware of this general latitude and pay as late as they can, knowing they will still receive the discount. You could ask your credit control department for a report of those customers who are pushing their luck a little too far and write to them pointing out the error of their ways. The cash discount is at your expense so you must ensure that the money is being wisely spent.

3. Cost discounts allowed into your selling price □

When calculating your selling prices add on a mark-up to cover the cost of cash discounts. If you look at your costing sheets you will no doubt find many items costed accurately but individually adding up to less than the cost of cash discount. Make sure you are using the correct factor for your discount levels.

4. Make customers aware of your payment terms □

Attractive settlement discounts can help to secure business, so ensure that your customers are aware of this important benefit. By doing so you may be sowing the seeds for prompt payment.

5. Make the exact payment date known □

When you raise the invoice you should be precise about the payment date rather than generalising about the terms. On the face of the invoice you could specify, for example, 'This invoice is due for payment on 28-10-19XX. After deducting cash discount the net sum payable is £.... No cash discount will be allowed on payment received after this date.'

6. Ensure that sales staff understand the payment terms □

It is surprising how many don't know – they think cash discounts are for the accounts people. Make sure they understand your payment terms – it may help to win an extra order or two.

7. Vetting of new orders by credit control □

This is an excellent (and timely) opportunity to check the creditworthiness of new customers and also to press old customers for payment of earlier bills. An early vetting of customers' references, credit limits and orders received may save a lot of unnecessary expense.

8. Authorising the despatch of an order by credit control □

During the time between receipt of an order and its execution or despatch the client's creditworthiness or payment history may have worsened, so a final check may be worth your while. Your lawyer may be able to advise you regarding transfer of title to the goods; you may be able to hold on to the legal title to the goods until you receive payment in full, even though the goods have been physically handed over.

9. Invoice on time □

Invoicing should take place as soon as the order is executed, not weeks later. If you send invoices promptly you stand a better chance of getting paid on time. All your billing paperwork should be up-to-date as any delay could mean you miss your customer's cheque-run and have to wait for the next. Don't think that because there are, say, 50 days between invoice and due date, there is no hurry. All companies 'systemise' their payments and the earlier your invoice gets into the system, the faster you are likely to be paid.

10. Send statements out on time □

Once again, as with invoices, a late statement may mean you miss that all-important cheque-run.

11. Involve sales staff in problem solving □

Sometimes a minor problem holds up payment but no one wants to get involved–especially the sales staff. This probably leaves your credit control department trying to solve problems and they may well not be the best people to do so. Sales staff, on the other hand, may have more detailed knowledge of a complaint, so they must help wherever they can.

12. Withhold sales people's commission in respect of late and non-payments □

By doing this, those niggling problems may be solved more promptly by the field staff.

13. Start the cash collection drive before the due payment date □

Make contact with your client's accounts department before the due date, making it known in the politest way possible that the payment date is imminent. This way your payment may arrive on time.

14. Chase big debts before small ones □

Twenty per cent of your customers probably account for 80 per cent of your debts. Concentrate on these first: they are more harmful to your business.

15. Personalise debt collection □

Many companies send standard stereotyped or photocopied letters demanding payment, but these often go straight into the waste-paper basket. Your credit controller should get to know his opposite number whenever he can. The person writing out the cheques may put yours in the system a little earlier if he feels he knows you. A good rapport between accounts departments can be helpful.

16. Push ahead with the collection procedure after your patience is exhausted □

Delays caused by not having an established procedure in the later stages of debt collection could prove critical and damaging. It is at the later stages of the debt collection procedure that the risk of a bad debt is greater, so being organised, including pressing for payment through legal channels, is essential.

17. Ask for a deposit with the order or for part or full payment prior to despatch □

This may be a way of helping with your cash flow crisis.

18. Issue pro-formas for slow payers and new accounts □

Insist on payment in advance for customers with a bad payment record and for new accounts.

19. Protect yourself against the risk of loss through late or non-payment of an export debt □

Check your payment terms for export orders on receipt of the order and again before execution and despatch. Check the validity and terms of your letter of credit and make sure that you have current Export Credits Guarantee Department (ECGD) cover where appropriate.

20. Bank all incoming cheques immediately □

Cheques are sometimes delayed in the accounts department while staff identify the payment against invoices. Why not photostat the cheque and bank the original without delay?

21. Demand payment of debit balances in the nominal, bought and other ledgers □

Some debtors' accounts are not maintained in the receivables ledger and can miss the credit controller's scrutiny. These 'special' accounts such as VAT, insurance claims etc, could add up to quite a lot of money. Debit balances in the bought ledger should be collected and not suspended to be offset against future purchases.

Chapter 2

Financial Awareness

1. Keep your employees informed ☐

Don't keep everyone totally in the dark – people like to know how the company is doing. If they know enough of the facts they will respond to the challenge of the company's policies.

2. Publicise financial targets ☐

Whatever your business you will have to work within certain financial constraints and towards some financial targets. Let the relevant employees down the line understand clearly what part they have to play in containing the business within these constraints.

3. Have a clear, straightforward financial control system ☐

Some control and information systems can be quite baffling to managers. Just because they are brilliant engineers it doesn't mean they understand figures. The financial information must be presented in a manner that can be understood by the non-accountant. Too many facts can confuse. So ensure that the system can be genuinely understood by those concerned. Keep it fairly straightforward and avoid technical terminology. Remember that the control system is intended to assist in the efficient running of the business. It should not be so complicated that it creates misunderstanding and mistrust.

4. Keep up-to-date with the reporting systems ☐

An extended time lag between the event and the reporting of the event so severely dilutes the impact of the report that it can have almost no effect. Reporting systems are a vital means of cost control and performance appraisal, and must be up-to-date.

5. Advance the report so as to anticipate adverse variances □

If all your control procedures are based on the recording of history it is rather like shutting the stable door after the horse has bolted. Where possible, devise a method of forecasting variances and taking evasive action in good time. Try analysing purchase orders, as opposed to purchase invoices, over their cost centres and you will anticipate excess costs. Also calculate the excess cost of an overtime programme before it is carried out rather than after the wages have been paid. By doing this on an *ad hoc* basis you may assist managers in avoiding the creation of adverse variances.

6. Improve the level of financial awareness □

As a business needs to respond to a continually changing series of events, it is vital for management to be aware of the financial implications. The overall target may remain un-altered, but tactics change by the minute. The wisest course of action is close liaison between finance staff and management if profit-responsible managers are to have the advice they need.

7. Organise an effective management audit □

While you're busy directing and controlling operations, an objective appraisal by an independent management auditor can help to crystallise objectives for improvement. Don't let him be simply a 'judge': he should be used positively, not merely as a critical observer.

8. Make the most effective use of your external auditors □

Usually very experienced and astute, the auditor can advise on financial matters in a constructive and dispassionate way. Use your auditors well and take advantage of their knowledge and experience.

9. Insist that the finance department is the pulse of the business □

A genuinely lively accounting staff that gets involved with events as and when they happen rather than a few reporting weeks later can act as a creative influence in minute-by-minute decision making. Trained accountants who get immersed in the running of the business can turn out to be the managers of the future.

10. Issue daily key statistics to managers □

Get your accounts department to circulate key statistics each day. Such statistics could include values of orders received, production and sales, cash balances, debtors and creditors etc. These would not be in the form of management accounts but should be viewed as an early warning system. Consider what are the main financial goals and criteria and monitor your achievement daily.

Chapter 3

Postage

Many businesses leave control of postage matters in the hands of a junior, but things may have gone wrong, so a speedy check on the post room cost-effectiveness wouldn't come amiss.

1. Supervise the outgoing mail □

In the last-minute dash to get everything in the post each night you may be incurring an extra cost here and there that you could avoid. Aim to reduce your postage bill by 10 per cent and you will get the benefit of that saving for ever. Check the contents and the cost of the outgoing mail, remembering that every morning you probably discard at least 10 per cent of your incoming mail as unimportant. Similarly, 10 per cent of your outgoing mail may end up in the recipients' waste-paper baskets, unread and unnoticed.

2. Check postal scales for accuracy □

If your scale is overweighing you're paying more for postage than you need.

3. Send mail out at the correct rate □

Post Office charges vary according to type, distance, weight, speed and method of delivery. Someone in the firm should be aware of the current rates and ensure that the postal service is being used to its full economic advantage.

4. Combine postings to avoid duplication of postage costs □

You possibly have a bank of regular customers or suppliers to whom letters, invoices, statements, cheques, acknowledgements, etc are regularly sent. It may be worth your while to try to coincide these mailings, thus saving postage and envelopes.

5. Use second-class mail □

It may seem trivial but work it out. Mail sent second class costs about 20 per cent less so should be used in preference to first class when there is no great urgency.

6. Make maximum use of outgoing mail □

Many firms now send sales brochures and special offers or news bulletins with their invoices and statements. Use this opportunity, as most incoming mail gets sent to the right department on receipt, regardless of the envelope's varied contents.

7. Combine mailings to branches, area staff etc □

Get each department to put such mail into the pigeon hole so that the post room can put all items for a common address into one envelope only. Separately posted letters to the same address cost money and make you look inefficient in the eyes of the recipient.

8. Pay the lowest prices for parcel post □

Get quotations from the many overnight, fast, door-to-door delivery services now available.

9. Make use of Post Office special deals □

First-class letter contracts and the second-class discount service for pre-sorted letters, with 4000 or more mailed at any one time, offer discounts from 10 per cent upwards.

For bulk mailing of pre-sorted mail, where items are of the same shape, size and weight, with delivery up to seven working days after posting being acceptable, discounts range from 10 per cent on 4000 minimum despatch to 30 per cent on a million or more.

If you spend more than £20,000 a year on inland letter postage, you may qualify for an incentive discount on percentage growth in postal expenditure.

Chapter 4

Telephones

Long telephone conversations are obviously expensive. Calls should be planned and precise but, in addition to keeping the conversation as short as possible, consider other ways of reducing the telephone bill.

1. Check for overcharges on your telephone bill □

By keeping a close eye on all the detail and by checking against your own records it may surprise you how often you may be able to identify an overcharge. Perhaps you don't even look at the telephone bill but please don't leave it to the telephone company. Treat it like any other supplier's invoice and subject the account to scrutiny. Get out the last three years' telephone bills and compare the quarterly charges item by item, line by line.

2. Meter the cost of telephone calls □

If you don't have a call logger have a chat with your operator to see who spends too much time on the phone – then confront the culprits frankly.

3. Make use of cheap and standard rate calls □

British Telecom's charges vary according to distance and the time of day the call is made. For example, 'cheap rates' are available Monday to Friday 6 to 8 pm and weekends, 'standard rates' Monday to Friday 8 to 9 am and 1 to 6 pm, and 'peak rates' are Monday to Friday 9 am to 1 pm.

Calls made during cheap rate times are less than half the cost of peak rate calls, and those made during standard rate times are generally a quarter to a third less than the cost of peak rate calls.

Every business should obtain a copy of the booklet 'Your guide to telephone charges' obtainable free of charge from British Telecom, and study it. By retiming routine calls and properly controlling the use of the telephone in your business your telephone costs will plummet.

4. Discourage reverse charge calls ☐

Very expensive. Get your operator to make a note of the number and return the call.

5. Make staff aware of your firm's telephone account ☐

Make them aware of the cost and they'll most likely want to co-operate to reduce it.

6. Lock direct lines at night ☐

You are inviting private calls by employees working late, particularly those expensive overseas calls, if you don't lock each extension that has an outside line. Simple locks are available.

7. Pay a fair proportion of home telephone accounts ☐

A number of executives have all or part of their home telephone accounts paid by the company, usually because they use their home phones for business in the evenings and at weekends. You should check that you are not paying too big a share. If the employees' contribution was fixed years ago it could be adjusted for inflation.

8. Plan the conversation ☐

As time is most definitely money when it comes to the telephone, outgoing calls should be planned. Prepare the call by making a note of what you want to say, getting the relevant files out and knowing the right reference numbers, extension number etc. Searching for information while the call charge is ticking away is pure waste.

9. Book calls through the operator □

Some people book their calls through a secretary, who in turn processes the call through the operator. Try asking the operator to get your calls directly for you, leaving your secretary free to do some important work in a different capacity.

10. Wait for the call to come through □

Stay at your desk until the call comes through. If you disappear the call charge is still ticking away. Nothing irritates the person at the other end more than hanging on for an incoming call.

11. Make maximum use of operator time □

The operator is probably very busy at peak times but not so busy at other times. He or she may be busy for only 50 per cent of the time and may like to take on additional work for off-peak times.

12. Get the telephone company to review your equipment requirements □

Many users have systems that were installed years, if not decades, ago. In the meantime there has been an explosion in communications technology and the requirements of your business may have changed. New equipment may be cheaper and may well require fewer operators.

13. Choose the right size switchboard □

More communications are through the telex and fax these days so you may have a telephone system too big for your requirements. A smaller board may cost less to rent or buy.

14. Cut down the number of extensions □

Everyone who uses the phone in the normal course of their job will need their own extension, but look at convenience extensions – by removing some your quarterly rental charge could be reduced. Also, limit the number of extensions on which overseas calls can be made.

15. Eliminate the internal telephone system □

The latest equipment can act as both external and internal communication. Save the duplicated rental costs and you may also avoid committing your company to an internal telephone system with a penal termination clause.

16. Give the best possible impression □

The telephone operator is often the first contact the caller has with the firm. This first contact must make a good impression, as people are always annoyed by an off-hand telephone reception. A helpful and efficient telephonist who responds in a bright and cheerful way can really contribute to the firm's image of quality and service. On the other hand, a bad telephonist can lose customers and that results in lost income.

The worst aspect of this is that you will probably never find out about it. So don't take any chances. Whenever you are out of the office, make a point of ringing in and see what kind of service you get. If it's bad for you it will be bad for your customers – or ex-customers. Ensure that your telephone operator is well trained and understands this point very clearly. He or she will appreciate your observations and will want to try to improve the firm's image as much as possible.

17. Make maximum use of the telex and fax □

Telex and telefax are generally much cheaper because the message is condensed and transmitted at a fast constant speed. They take less of your time and usually attract an immediate response from the receiver.

Chapter 5

Paper, Stationery and Office Sundries

1. Minimise your stationery stocks □

You probably have several stationery stores. People hoard paper, stationery and office sundries. Get them to have a big turn-out, and see how many pens, pencils, rubbers, clips and stapling machines they are hoarding. Then collect everything together and put it back into your office stationery stores. The same applies to letterheads, envelopes, photocopying paper etc. You could quite easily find that you have one or two months' stationery purchases in stock around the offices, plus another two or three months' in the stores. So why not get it under better control (you may even find you don't have to buy stationery and sundries for a couple of months)?

2. Stationery purchasing by a trained buyer □

Some companies leave stationery buying to a secretary or senior clerk. However, there is much more to buying than placing orders with the same supplier. One of your buying staff may make a sizeable impression on your purchase prices, obtaining competitive quotations and considering contracts with large quantity discounts.

3. Control the consumption of pens, pencils, erasers etc □

You'll find you're supplying these items to half the neighbourhood. Pens, pencils etc just drift into other people's hands, so limit their issue and you'll save expense.

4. Consolidate forms □

If you can put two internal reports on to one sheet you will halve the amount of paper, photocopying and messenger time etc without reducing the amount or value of the information.

5. Control the use of the photocopier □

Uncontrolled use of the photocopier can lead to abuse. However, employing a full-time operator can also be expensive. Keep a watchful eye on photocopier use and make sure you don't have a queue of staff watching the operator at work.

6. Restrict the number of internally circulated copies □

See if you can reduce the number of copies being circulated. Apart from the cost of the paper etc, it involves the recipients in a lot of reading time which perhaps could be more wisely used.

7. Reduce the amount of photocopying paper being used □

Use both sides where possible and use a larger paper size to copy two or more documents at the same time.

8. Avoid using photocopying paper for internal and less important documentation □

Cheaper quality paper can be as little as half the cost.

9. Appreciate the cost of computer stationery □

Find out how much computer stationery costs and you'll soon reduce the mass of computer reporting that takes place.

10. Use the appropriate printer ribbon □

Use carbon ribbons in your computer printer where a very high standard of presentation is essential. Reusable ribbons are adequate for less important documents.

11. Type on both sides of file copy paper □

Fifty per cent of the cost will be saved.

12. Address envelopes as cheaply as possible □

Remember window envelopes? Or use a word processor to store and retrieve your mailing list, then print out on to adhesive labels.

13. Check waste-paper baskets □

Have a look at the contents of waste-paper baskets in order to identify excess wastage generally.

14. Dispose of filed information when it is no longer needed □

If it's not required by statute and if you'll never need to refer to it, then get rid of it and save space, heating, lighting, rates and filing cabinets. Have each file that goes into the archives marked with the date on which the file contents can be destroyed. At the same time put the old file back into circulation with a new heading.

Before you place anything into your filing system first consider whether or not you really wish to retain that information. You may save the equivalent of at least one person's time now spent on unnecessary filing.

15. Pay less for your office furniture □

Look around your offices and you will see many desks, chairs and so on in good condition that are several years old. Before you buy a new desk etc for your new branch or new employee take a look at the second-hand office furniture market, or alternatively, consider refurbishing existing furniture. A coat of paint will be much cheaper.

Chapter 6

Internal Communications and Meetings

Some businesses reach the size or position where a great deal of internal communication and contact are necessary. Hand in hand with the increase in necessary internal communication grows a plethora of less necessary and even superfluous communication. A business may reach a stage where the extent of internal communication and reporting has got out of hand.

1. Eliminate unnecessary internal communication and reporting □

People could be asking for information for the sake of it. It may take five minutes to read a report but it may take the writer and secretary hours or even days of research to produce it. They are expensive people – don't waste their time.

2. Consider the cost of producing a report □

Calculate the relevant manager's hourly rate and overheads, including a secretary and other members of staff, and evaluate the cost of producing reports. Then think whether their time could have been more wisely spent or whether you really need them for that purpose.

3. Avoid becoming too insular in your work routines □

People can become part of an elaborate overhead structure completely divorced from the real business activities of the company. Ask whether this structure is really needed or whether the relevant people could do something more useful.

4. Save typing time by using handwritten internal memoranda ☐

Get everyone to handwrite internal memos on self-carbonising paper. The number and size of these communications will reduce dramatically.

5. Audit the need for regular reports ☐

On the next issue of any of these reports that you send, pin a note saying that you will not send further issues unless the recipient requests it. You may find half the people on the circulation list don't reply. Not only do they not read your report, they may not even have noticed the note you pinned on it.

6. Control the number of meetings ☐

Check that meetings are attended only by those who really need to attend; check they are all called for a worthwhile purpose, and that they are properly prepared. Target yourself to reduce the number and length of meetings by 75 per cent. Forbid any meetings at all on three days a week and start meetings in the late afternoon.

7. Make sales conferences worthwhile ☐

Before you hold the next one, check the minutes of the past three meetings, see how repetitive they are and how few or how many decisions are actioned successfully. Don't hold the next meeting until satisfactory progress has been made, otherwise those attending may become cynical about the conference value.

8. Select meeting centres ☐

It is often the custom to bring territory staff to headquarters to attend sales conferences or training sessions. Depending on the location of HQ you might be better off relocating your conferences out of town. Don't have your conferences based where hotels, travel, food and parking are the most expensive. Base them out of town, choose a centre geared to the location of your outside staff and branches, and cut the cost by half.

9. Time meetings sensibly ☐

Arrange your business conferences to coincide with an exhibition which the same staff may have to attend for stand manning – avoid duplicating travel time and costs.

10. Limit the length of union meetings ☐

Be firm, cut them short where possible, and if the answer has to be negative don't beat about the bush – there's work to be done.

Chapter 7

Advertising

Expenditure on advertising etc is very often simply a matter of personal judgement. You can argue for more expenditure; you can argue for less expenditure. You can argue that the recent advertising spree has resulted in more sales; you can argue that greater advertising would have increased sales even further. The advertising budget is a subjective decision, but the publicity and advertising staff are certainly capable of achieving high spending levels. Ask yourself the question: Would I have made more profit if I had spent less on advertising?

1. Keep a special watch on the big spenders in the camp □

If your company has a big spender, he could well be in the publicity department. It may not be his fault, however, because he is often under pressure from all sides to improve the company's image. Because of this pressure the publicity budget is often overspent, so a firm resolve to keep within budget is needed.

2. Spend less on advertising in slack times □

Some people spend more money on advertising when business is slack in the hope that it will create a greater demand. First, find out why you are slack. Is it because the overall market is lower but nevertheless you are maintaining your market share, or is it because your competitors are outperforming you? Before you advertise more, put your house in order.

3. Take advantage of local events to obtain local publicity ☐

Try sponsoring a major local event in the area concerned, such as a carnival, sports event or charity effort using uniforms, posters, programmes, acknowledgements on the public address system etc. This gets your products and name in the public eye.

4. Send regular editorial matter to the trade and technical press ☐

Editorial matter sometimes makes more impact on the reader than an advertisement. There are often so many advertisements in a magazine or publication that few readers will notice yours. This results in the advertisers trying to out-advertise each other, which may be good business for the publication but is it any good for you? Come up with lots of good stories for the press.

5. Have an open day for the press ☐

Just occasionally you may have the opportunity to invite the press to your open day – perhaps for the launch of a new product or for your company's centenary or a major export order. Make a good day of it: invite as many people as possible to attend and give them personal attention. You're bound to get a write-up (usually a quote from your well prepared press hand-out) as the journalists have to report on their day out – and in any case you've had a good story to tell.

6. Circulate press cuttings on your company to your customers and sales staff ☐

The exercise isn't over when you've got a story in print. Everyone is impressed with printed matter about someone they know and it will boost the confidence of your sales staff and customers. Your employees and suppliers will also be impressed – they're important too.

7. Spend less on each advert □

It is not always the most expensive, full colour, double-page advertisement that makes the best impression. See how much cheaper a smaller and less frequent advertisement would be. People are sometimes very vulnerable in front of an advertising agent and the company may become committed to a major advertising splash for the wrong reason.

8. Negotiate advertising rates □

Perhaps your buying office can help you to get better rates. They are used to hard bargaining.

9. Reuse existing artwork □

Artwork is very expensive and money can be saved by a re-run of previous advertisements. Keep your artwork safe.

10. Curtail your advertising agent's spending □

An agent makes more money, the more you spend. He'll be happy if you go for a bigger, more expensive, more frequent advertising campaign. It could be worth monitoring that expenditure does not exceed the agreed budget figure.

11. Buy publicity-related services direct from the supplier □

Advertising agents will usually make a profit on any service, however small, that they arrange for you. Search for opportunities to go direct for some of these services. In quiet times you may well have the capacity to do the work yourself.

12. Update your mailing list □

It may be costing a pretty penny sending news bulletins, advertising information etc to companies or people who no longer exist or, if they do, no longer play a significant role in your company's activities. Put a return address on your envelopes to increase the chance of undelivered items coming back to you.

13. Control the issue of give-aways □

Unless they're good they won't be well received. Check that they're necessary in order to get more business.

14. Limit the number of Christmas gifts you hand out □

Be very careful about whom you give Christmas gifts to. You never know what petty jealousy they may be creating and unless you hand them out personally there is a chance that the wrong person will receive the gift. If you make a definite rule not to give company presents at Christmas you may save a lot of aggravation as well as money.

15. Analyse the effectiveness of advertising □

By putting a reference on the reply coupon contained in your advertisement you can identify which magazines, which issue etc produced the best response, not only as to quantity but also quality. In later advertising campaigns, eliminate those magazines which gave a poor response.

16. Advertising by direct mail □

There are firms which can give you lists of almost everything – builders, farmers, garden centres etc. Such lists detail the full names, addresses and telephone numbers and can be analysed by area, type, size etc. Coupled with the use of the latest word processing equipment, they enable you to contact the customer directly by name.

17. Advertising by telephone □

Like direct mail this form of communication has a better chance of making contact with the person at whom the advertising is aimed. It also gives an opportunity for feedback and can be quite cost-effective.

18. Share the cost of an advert ☐

If your firm provides a product or service as a constituent part of a product or service in which others are involved, it may be in your interest to consider joint or shared advertising, eg the major suppliers to a construction project.

Chapter 8

Manning Strategy

You are doubtless very conscious of present-day employment costs. Every employee is costing you in salary or wage, plus the employer's National Insurance contribution, the employer's pension contribution, sick pay schemes, holiday pay, overalls, BUPA, company car, petrol etc. In addition, there are indirect costs incurred by every employee, in terms of supervision, incidental materials and equipment such as desk, work bench, telephone and so on.

Obviously, some employees can cost ten times as much as others. But even the cheapest employees are expensive if they are not being used to your best advantage.

1. Know how many people you employ □

If you don't know the answer, then your manning levels are almost certainly questionable. If you don't know the exact manning levels in your company or in the departments, or are out by as little as 1 per cent, it is possible that this matter is not under control. Existing manning levels are often accepted without question, whereas an adjustment up or down may be advantageous.

2. Ensure that departmental managers and supervisors at *all* levels know what their present manning levels and requirements are □

Present departmental manning levels may be simply the results of history, and not the effective planning of your true present-day requirements. You are likely to find that the majority of managers don't know the exact number they employ and some will get the answer wrong by as much as 20 per cent.

3. Account for every employee on the payroll ☐

It has been known for a non-existent Mr X to appear suddenly on a company's payroll. You thereby find yourself paying a wage to somebody who does not actually exist. Check physically the number of people you employ and compare this with your payroll. Have a change of supervisors or staff watching over the handing-out of wage packets. Take a personal interest in those packets which are not claimed by an individual at pay-out time and see that they are sent to a real person.

4. Monitor the numbers employed and their job categories ☐

See that you get a regular report in order to avoid a shock increase in the number employed.

5. Check that all jobs are really necessary ☐

Let's be honest – sometimes jobs are 'created'. They may have been 'created' some years ago when you could afford to be generous, but times and fortunes may have changed for your company since then. Now is the time to look at each of your employees and analyse their individual profit contribution.

6. Involve managers and supervisors at the various levels when manning reductions are needed ☐

It is possible that senior managers are unable to identify savings fully. They may make broad-brush policy decisions saying, for example, that reductions across the board need to be 10 per cent, and then leave it up to junior managers to comply with the decision. The lower grade managers may know better than the senior managers but are frequently not asked because it is a sensitive subject. Ask them for their views and assistance and you could find yourself making savings that you didn't expect. Some managers will be unhelpful, however, so you will have to be firmer with them.

7. Ask for voluntary staff reductions ☐

You may be able to obtain manpower reductions through volunteers.

8. Offer an early retirement scheme ☐

Some employees (not always those on the verge of retirement only) may welcome this opportunity.

9. Minimise the number of departments in the company ☐

Reorganising the management and departmental structure of your company can leave you with a more streamlined operation, requiring fewer departments and eliminating duplication of effort.

10. Minimise the number of people employed solely on internal matters ☐

Take a good look to see if all the internal work is really necessary.

11. Restrict overtime ☐

You should have a very thorough and detailed scrutiny of every single hour of overtime worked in your office, warehouse or factory. Overtime should be vetted and sanctioned daily by senior management. Overtime often becomes a habit.

12. Ask staff to work harder ☐

Employees can get into a rut. If approached sensibly and politely they may like to accept the challenge of taking on more work. Some employees become less enthusiastic about their work simply because they are bored, so additional work can give them new life.

13. Review remuneration methods ☐

By applying incentives to those departments where there is opportunity to do so, you may achieve an increase in productivity. Remember that an incentive scheme can be introduced on a temporary basis to meet a short-term increase in demand. Such an incentive should be on the basis of improved productivity, ie more output at less unit cost.

14. Check for wage drift ☐

Incentive schemes that have been in existence for a long time can often become slack and either intentionally or unintentionally abused. This causes an uncontrolled upward drift in wage costs.

15. Achieve an acceptable labour turnover rate ☐

Every time an employee leaves it costs money. Many employers feel that they have a satisfactory labour turnover ratio, but upon examination find that the labour turnover, although small overall, takes place mainly within one department or one particular group of employees. On this basis the departmental or employee group labour turnover ratio may be too high. It may be that two-thirds of the workforce give medium- to long-term service and one-third of the workforce have a very high turnover rate. Examine these incidences of high labour turnover and you may find an opportunity to reduce it by giving different rates of pay or by carrying out the work in a different and more acceptable manner.

16. Increase overtime for existing staff before taking on extra workers ☐

This keeps staff overheads down.

17. Review the need for part-timers ☐

Part-timers are usually employed when there is a temporary

increase in the workload. Unfortunately, they are sometimes kept on even when the workload reduces to its normal level.

18. Recruit part-time staff □

There are times when a part-timer is adequate for your needs. You obviously reduce wages by having fewer hours worked, but in addition you save National Insurance and other employee-related costs.

19. Recruit on a temporary basis when you need staff with a special skill □

For a specific job you may require a specific skill, but why take on a permanent member of staff with a particular skill which may only be needed for a short time? Hire your specialist skills as and when you need them. Retired people (very often below the official retiring age) may often be useful to carry out short-term special assignments.

20. Monitor waiting time □

Even a little waiting time or idle time is unacceptable. Define the reasons for this waste and organise your factory and office to eliminate it.

21. Have time sheets for office staff □

From time to time ask the office staff to fill in a time sheet for, say, a period of one month. From this time sheet you will be able to analyse which jobs are taking the greatest amount of time, and you can direct your managers towards improving the system so that these jobs are done more efficiently.

22. Take advantage of the revolution in automating office procedures □

The era of modern business machinery is here to stay and you will benefit by taking advantage of the latest office equipment available. Many of the hard slog, clerical jobs in your office can be done better and more efficiently with the new machinery. Many companies have improved manpower performance in the factory by purchasing new plant and machinery, but attention should now be turned to carrying out the same exercise on administrative procedures.

23. Reduce absenteeism □

Absenteeism usually results in overmanning. Perhaps you could adopt a firmer policy.

24. Identify poor performance □

A proportion of your workforce will be poor performers. The reasons for their poor performance will be many and may in fact result from poor management over the years. Nevertheless, you must never forget that poor performers cost you money and good performers make you money. Try to build a team of first-rate performers by encouraging the poor performers to improve.

25. Hire staff on short-term or temporary contracts □

To meet a temporarily increased workload you will probably find it more cost-effective to employ staff on a short-term basis or on a temporary contract. In this way you will not continue to incur their costs when the work peak falls.

26. Authorise any recruitment □

Insist on a simple discipline to authorise taking on new recruits. Before any such authorisation you can consider transferring surplus staff from one job to another.

27. Review the purpose of recruitment □

You need to ensure that employees, such as direct production workers, are not recruited for an important job and then transferred to less important work. Such a transfer may be of a temporary nature at the time it occurs, but becomes permanent by default and through lack of control. Some companies employ direct workers only to find that they are soon doing less and less direct work and more and more indirect work.

28. Screen new employees ☐

You should always obtain employer's and personal references by telephone if possible. The referee is less prepared than when answering a reference enquiry letter. You will get a more spontaneous and perhaps a more informative answer. (It may be necessary to send a letter in advance of your call to prove your bona fides.) This should result in more effective recruitment.

29. Retrain ☐

There could well be a reservoir of untapped expertise and ability in your company. Many people do not rise to the occasion unless you give them the occasion to rise to.

30. Make use of the Youth Training Scheme ☐

This is well worth looking into and you may find a very useful permanent employee in the process.

31. Authorise the employment of trainees ☐

Check exactly what the trainees are doing, as many managers feel that because someone is a trainee, it justifies their carrying out unimportant jobs. Get them on direct productive work.

Chapter 9

Remuneration Reviews

Gone are the days when you could automatically pass on cost increases to your customers through your product selling price. So it is essential that all increases in wages and salaries are justifiable, properly controlled and if possible self-financing.

1. Account for the total increase in your wages and salaries bill from one year to another ☐

Many companies find that the total wage bill can increase in a year by an amount far greater than the rate increase warrants. It would be wise to find out why there is such a discrepancy. Of course there are plenty of good reasons for wage drift but you should know what they are and then act to control the situation. The additional cost should be analysed into increases in rates, numbers employed, overtime worked, bonus earnings, changes in labour mix etc by age, grade and so on.

2. Monitor 'automatic' increases ☐

Increases in respect of age, length of service etc are usually automatic but nevertheless need controlling. Establish the cost of such increases and review the policy as necessary.

3. Manage the annual review ☐

An 'across the board' increase is usually the most straight-forward method of dealing with the annual pay round. Apart from the argument over the actual sums, it can be applied with the minimum of effort and fuss. However, a percentage increase on a rate of pay also affects holiday pay, overtime pay, pensions, national insurance etc so, although a simple method, the 'across the board' increase can be very expensive.

4. Be discerning with the annual review □

The annual review tends to ignore the fact that some employees deserve more and some less than others. High performers can in effect be penalised because of low performers who are given the same increase. To compensate for this apparent unfairness, merit rises can be given selectively but the result is that the total cost of the annual review is much higher.

5. Relate the annual increase to a generally higher performance □

Performance related increases are the most cost-effective. If a pay increase stimulates improved productivity and is self-financing you will be more competitive and improve your profit margins.

6. Assess employee performance □

Some company departments contain staff who, being slightly less self-motivated than others, tend steadily to pursue their allotted task without too much enthusiasm and initiative. Unfortunately the manager turns a blind eye and everyone becomes too contented. Nobody recognises the plight of the individual, who gives up trying. So look around – you may have latent talent that just needs encouragement. Convert more of your staff into high performance employees, give them more work and watch them lap it up – they'll begin to feel important again. Talk to your staff; jointly assess their performance and determine how they can be more effective.

7. Review incentive schemes □

Payment by results methods of remuneration are often open

to a little manipulation and, as methods of production change, the 'incentive' aspect of the payments scheme diminishes. So take a look at your scheme: if it has been in use for some time it's probably long overdue for a change.

8. Staff participation in the profits of the company □

Whereas the sales staff and production workers are rewarded according to their efforts, other staff are often excluded from any incentive or profit sharing scheme. Some form of profit share can be an excellent motivation.

9. Maintain a fair pay structure □

So often we find people in junior and middle management earning less than, say, a production worker on an incentive scheme or a commission earning sales person. Overtime pay for hourly paid staff but not for the salaried production engineering staff or foremen also creates serious injustices which can demoralise someone who has made what is possibly a greater contribution to the company's results.

Chapter 10

Legal Costs

At some point you may receive a bill for legal costs that seems staggeringly out of proportion to what you had originally envisaged. Unless you keep a close watch on the situation you may find that, having put a certain matter into the legal system, the various aspects that can be pursued soon add up to a heavy bill. Having started on this process, it may become difficult to back out, with the result that, what was at first deemed to be a fairly minor exercise develops into a campaign, each stage of which incurs more cost.

So, we should judge the merits of taking legal action or of using the services of the legal profession in the same commercial way that we would purchase other goods or services for the company. Unfortunately we don't usually do this because we just don't know what is going on behind the legal scenes. Consequently, we tend to accept professional charges as being fair for the job carried out, relying on the solicitor or lawyer to invoice according to the time and costs he incurs on our problem.

1. Use more than one firm of legal advisers □

Some of your legal work can be done by local solicitors, whereas the more specialised work may have to be carried out by a large city firm. Generally, the bigger firms are more expensive so you could select your advisers according to the complexity of the task.

2. Educate your lawyer □

The closer you are to your solicitor the more easily you can learn from him just what the legal steps he is taking for you imply in terms of costs. Some firms of lawyers seem to live in ivory towers so make an effort to get to know him better; this will certainly benefit you. Bring him to your office or works, show him round and encourage his interest in your firm generally.

3. Assess the fee implications of your instructions ☐

If you are running your firm as financially effectively as you can, there can be few decisions made whose financial effects you do not consider. You should ask your lawyer what alternative courses of action are available to you and how much they will cost. Then you will be able to judge the cost-effectiveness of your decision.

4. Systemise your legal work ☐

Some legal work (for example, the collection of debts through legal channels) can be systemised so as to reduce administrative effort in your firm and by your solicitor. Such streamlining of the routines could result in cost savings. If the information is prepared and presented clearly and concisely to your solicitor, then he may save his time and your costs.

5. Obtain estimates or quotations for legal work ☐

By putting your legal work out for quotation you will very quickly identify cost savings. Also you will spot those firms who are keen for business, with the possible consequences that they may be able to act more quickly.

6. Check the reasonableness of your lawyer's bill ☐

Query his account as a matter of routine. It will show that you are keeping a check on his charges and may influence him towards keeping them as low as possible.

7. Negotiate lawyers' bills ☐

It's really just straightforward good buying practice.

8. Analyse itemised legal bills ☐

Legal work can be of varying complexity and can be carried out by junior or senior members of staff. So why pay a flat rate or a lump sum?

9. Authorisation of legal bills by head office staff ☐

Branch or departmental staff may have a less inquisitive approach to legal bills. They could be mesmerised by legal jargon. Use your HO expertise and experience.

10. Independent checking of legal bills ☐

Firms that have in-house lawyers often let the company lawyer agree the charges from outside firms. Let your purchasing director pass these bills through rigorous buying office routines.

Chapter 11

Travel

Markets are becoming more international, distances are shrinking, more and more executives travel more frequently on overseas trips; travel expenditure is an area of potential waste that once brought under control, can significantly reduce your cost burden. Both national and inter-national travel costs need regular scrutiny.

1. Check the necessity for the journey □

Check the reason for a journey, check that it has been planned properly and that there are clear new objectives. Check that existing objectives cannot be attained by means of cheaper communication such as telex, telephone or fax.

2. Keep car travel down □

If someone travels 300 miles in a round trip it will take pretty well all day. One call in the middle of the journey may prove to be productive but don't forget that the other seven or eight hours' driving has achieved very little. So plan journeys in such a way that the maximum benefit is gained from the time spent behind the wheel.

3. Choose a reasonably priced hotel □

Owing to the development of national and international hotel chains, businessmen tend to select one particular group, perhaps because of its high standard of communication and service. But this can be very expensive. By selecting a less prestigious hotel, the money saved can pay for an extended stay or a return trip. Many country hotels offer very good home comforts and service at a quarter of the price.

4. Choose the right accommodation for the employee ☐

Hotel selection should depend upon the job the member of staff will perform. There is obviously a minimum standard that should apply to all employees but, beyond that, any increment in cost due to higher standards should be justified according to the extra facilities the job requires. If it is a question of a quick overnight stay, breakfast in the morning and away to work by 7.30 am, there is no point in paying a room rate that includes something for the use of the swimming pool, tennis court, sauna etc. Longer stays, where your hotel is your office base and where you effectively set up home for a few weeks, may well justify the higher room rates.

5. Choose the location of your hotel carefully ☐

Occasionally the location of a hotel can cause you to spend more on travel, eg taxis to and from your clients' offices.

6. Negotiate discounts for hotels ☐

Most hotel groups offer group discounts. However, be aware that the discounted rate may still exceed the rates of alternative acceptable hotels. The discount *per se* is not justification for using a particular hotel chain.

7. Compare the cost of hotel meals with local restaurants ☐

Once in a hotel don't let yourself become a captive diner who pays through the nose for hotel meals. Down the road you may get as good a meal in very comfortable surroundings for half the price.

8. Observe the cost of hotel telephones ☐

Some hotels charge a high premium for use of the telephone. Telephone costs are high enough anyway so don't add to them by paying an enormous premium to the hotel.

9. Use credit cards □

When you take travellers' cheques the cost is debited from your bank account before you actually spend the money. By using credit cards (carefully controlled) you pay for your travel expenses several weeks later.

10. Pay employees' credit card subscription charges □

By your paying the annual fee, the employee can afford to have at least one credit card to which his expenses can be charged. The employee will find this more convenient but of course his claim for expenses will go through your normal scrutiny. In the meantime your company has saved bank interest.

11. Employ more than one travel agent □

Some firms get locked in to one travel agent, but by giving them a monopoly you could be the loser. Go to several travel agents to get comparative quotes for the same journey. Then you will see just how complex air fare structures can be and how a travel agent with a competitive spirit can save you a small fortune. In-house travel offices give good service but are they working as competitively as they can in a non-competitive environment?

12. Plan overseas trips □

Overseas travel is so expensive that the maximum amount of planning should go into each trip. How often have you seen export sales executives sitting around waiting in the hotel foyer for their contact to arrive? Perhaps the reason for his delay is that your agent is out making last-minute appointments around town – a job which should have been done weeks ahead.

13. Understand air fare structures □

With so many different structures available, eg first class, club class, economy, tourist, APEX, standby and many more, you should perhaps have someone in your organisation who is really familiar with these various fares schemes. Buying travel is a specialist function, so train the person responsible in your company to do the job really well.

14. Save by buying air tickets overseas □

If one of your staff regularly visits a particular area ask him to compare the cost of purchasing a ticket there. He can use a credit card for the payment and in some instances will make very large savings indeed. A 12-month ticket is purchased at home for the first trip and the final return trip but in between trips are bought overseas. Alternatively, cheaper one-way flights may be available in the country of destination. In some instances savings can be made by buying locally any internal and onward overseas flights. Use your sales executives to find out about these cost reducing opportunities.

15. Make use of airport hotels □

If meetings involve air travel, ask your customers, suppliers or employees to hold the meeting at the airport hotel. This saves the expense of driving into town and possibly an overnight stop.

16. Maintain performance throughout the duration of the trip □

So often you see sales people going through the motions of selling, but getting nowhere. They busy themselves from plane to plane, from hotel to hotel, from taxi to taxi and from office to office – but end up unsuccessful. Consider the various factors that can influence the success or failure of a trip – lack of time, lack of planning, lack of follow-up, lack of energy resulting from an overpacked itinerary. Make sure you give enough time to the job in hand, set your sights firmly on your target and sit tight. Give enough time to follow up and close the deal.

17. Provide adequate back-up □

It is so frustrating to be at the sharp end fighting for a contract, only to be let down by the office. Set up a proper communication arrangement that supplies back-up information seven days a week to your export sales staff. Remember they may well be working while you are sleeping, having a weekend off or a national holiday.

18. Open doors □

Especially in the Middle East and Far East you will need a high status to open the doors of business opportunity. A single visit by the chief executive can lead to lots of business in the future and can make ensuing overseas travel by junior staff much more effective.

Chapter 12

Company Cars

1. Operate the minimum number of company cars □

Cars are expensive, so keep the numbers down.

2. Provide employees with a fair quality car □

According to status, employees are allocated a 'grade' of car.
Be careful that the grading doesn't drift upwards as car manufacturers improve their specification year by year.

3. Obtain the best trade-in values □

Many fleet owners dispose of their cars through auctions but it
may be possible for a higher price to be obtained on a private
sale basis.

4. Look at the second-hand market for your vehicle requirements □

Low mileage used cars are often available at a very much
lower price.

5. Carry out in-house servicing and repairs □

Your own maintenance department may well be qualified to
carry out this work.

6. Control the amount of private mileage □

Check the proportion of private to business mileage and
reduce excess use for private purposes. There is perhaps no

need to be unreasonable but some degree of restraint is needed in order to be fair to all car users and to protect the company's interests.

7. Contribution by employees for private use ☐

A nominal weekly contribution from each nominated driver can add up to a worthwhile annual total. Such a contribution could be in exchange for the privilege of using the car at weekends or for allowing family use.

8. Consider vehicle leasing ☐

This is often the most cost-effective method of vehicle financing.

9. Issue vehicle operators with credit cards ☐

It gives your company free credit for fuel purchases and this saves bank interest. It also makes accounting easier, but beware of misuse.

10. Record vehicle mileage and vehicle costs ☐

Be careful that you are not keeping a vehicle on the road that really needs to be replaced. Companies devise general policies that are not necessarily appropriate to all car users. For example a policy by which cars are changed every three years may be entirely unsuitable to a sales representative travelling long distances in a large territory.

11. Plan journeys ☐

Ensure the optimum use of every mile travelled by every vehicle in the fleet by insisting on the careful planning of all journeys.

Chapter 13

Establishment Costs

Most business overheads are related either to the level of business activity or to the size of the establishment. For example, selling costs such as travel, commissions and entertaining tend to vary with sales volumes, as do labour costs, carriage costs etc. Certain overheads tend to be more fixed and depend upon the size of the company's site or its factory, offices, branches etc. Example of these types of overhead would be rent, rates, water, heating, lighting, interest, property maintenance, cleaning, insurance, security, site supervision, site communication, materials handling and internal transport.

1. Control the size of the establishment □

Large-scale production brings certain economies with it especially in times of stability or growth, but in periods of retraction large-scale facilities can be too costly. Ensure that establishment costs are affordable for both high and low levels of activity.

2. Assess the minimum/optimum establishment size for your present activity level □

Firms often work with facilities which have grown over the years as demand has developed. But are they what you really need now and for the future? Assess your ideal facilities objectively and compare them with what you have at present; you will at least have a picture of the changes you might make.

3. Collate the total establishment costs of your business ☐

Have these calculated so that you can assess the relevance of these costs to your overall cost levels. The idea here is that you should analyse your expenses to see what costs are being incurred relative to your establishment size. Include those items which you may not at first recognise as being concerned with the establishment, such as internal transport, security etc as mentioned above.

4. Divide the total establishment costs into activity or cost centres ☐

By analysing total establishment costs over defined centres you can compare one with the other. This will lead you to determine which activity centres are more expensive to run than others.

5. Calculate the proportion of production to non-production areas ☐

See how much of your factory/warehouse complex is genuinely productive and how much is taken up by materials storage, obsolete machinery, corridors, passageways, partitions etc.

6. Determine value or performance levels for each of these activity or function centres ☐

Such performance evaluation can be measured in production values, number of staff, function performed etc, so that comparisons can be made between such centres in the form of ratios, eg:

- establishment cost per square metre;
- establishment cost per employee;
- establishment cost per unit of production.

This will identify those areas with unsatisfactorily high establishment costs compared with the area 'value' or 'performance'.

7. Reduce the establishment costs in an area of poor performance □

It may not be possible to change the physical layout of a factory but any reduction in establishment cost of any type in an area of unsatisfactory performance will be of benefit.

8. Increase performance or value level in such an area □

An alternative to cost reduction would be to increase the performance or value of an area by additional activities, more productive staff, new products etc.

9. Combine the activities of two or more areas into a single reduced space □

By condensing the activities into a smaller space, the less productive or valuable areas are more easily identified, enabling remedial action to be taken.

10. Review the size of an individual's or a department's office □

Spacious offices can be just too expensive. A manager may need a little extra space but have your offices become just a little too spacious? Not every office need be a conference room as well.

11. Merge the head office with another unit □

Factories outside the city centre may have surplus land or buildings which would enjoy lower establishment costs.

12. Reduce the number of branches □

Companies with selling branches dotted around the country have to move with changes in demand. You may have branches close to each other that could now be closed, again generating cash and reducing establishment costs.

13. Eliminate unnecessary partitions ☐

Factories and offices, particularly old ones, often have too many nooks and crannies, cubby holes and partitions. The more of these there are, the less visibility there is of personnel, stocks, machinery and production in general. Partitions and walls take up too much space.

14. Re-allocate space per department/function to save money ☐

Work carried out by separate departments could be merged following physical re-allocation of work areas. For example, a combined despatch/goods inwards department could be less costly.

15. Dispose of obsolete items ☐

Storing obsolete items in the stores and on the shop floor takes up costly factory and warehouse area.

16. Reduce non-production areas ☐

Materials storage can often be improved both in stores and on the shop floor by the use of shelving and racking. Remember that few of the establishment costs are related to the building's height. Rent and rates, heating etc are the same whether you use only the floor area or the whole height of a building.

17. Close departments or buildings ☐

Establishment costs of empty buildings are significantly reduced; there is no point in paying establishment costs for two buildings where only one is needed.

18. Sell company houses ☐

Company owned houses can be a liability in terms of maintenance and administration.

19. Sell off property ☐

Realisation of unwanted assets puts cash in the bank and reduces interest costs as well as reducing establishment costs.

20. Make best use of spare land ☐

If you see no use for some parcels of land in the near future, perhaps a site development programme could be of benefit. Either sell the surplus land or build factory/warehouse units to produce investment income.

21. Obtain income from an under-used social club or conference room ☐

Many works social clubs are only open one or two nights a week so there are plenty or opportunities for rental income at other times.

22. Let out vacated buildings on short- or medium-term rentals ☐

Many companies with larger than necessary sites have taken advantage of the boom in growth of small factory/warehouse complexes. There is no need to make long-term arrangements with tenants but letting has two benefits, namely that someone else is paying for the establishment costs and you are receiving rental income.

23. Adopt a maintenance-free property policy ☐

This should be considered whenever possible, as the cost of maintenance is exorbitant. Carpets instead of floor tiles, aluminium window frames instead of steel or wood etc all reduce the maintenance and cleaning bill.

24. Reduce your property maintenance bill ☐

Maintenance programmes such as painting, decorating,

cleaning etc may be costing more than you can afford; it may be possible to postpone them.

25. Appeal against your rating assessment ☐

Rateable values have often been established for many years but the circumstances may have changed since they were set.

26. Influence the fixing of the rate with the local authority ☐

If you do not lobby your local and county councils you cannot influence the rate. Consequently it is assumed that you will pay whatever is decided by councils, so get involved and influence decisions so that the rate increases are affordable.

27. Compare the cost of your water rates with measured usage ☐

Water charges on a metered basis may be less expensive.

You will see from the foregoing suggestions that there is plenty of scope for improving profitability as a result of such an appraisal. Consider your office, factory and branches in the same way as the large retail shops look at use of their floor area. Set targets for earning a minimum contribution per square metre of land, or production or office area. The word 'establishment' implies a degree of permanence or inability to change, but this need not be the case.

Review the whole matter with a fresh approach, be flexible in your thinking and find new ways of getting to grips with those ever-increasing establishment costs.

Chapter 14

Energy Costs

Since the energy crisis of the early seventies to which management responded by reducing consumption to compensate for
increased prices, there appears to be comparative price
stability, resulting in a relaxation of pressure on energy conservation programmes. But management should not forget
two important facts:

1. Energy costs are still high.
2. There will be a further crisis as resources dry up.

In many factories and offices energy costs are still quite high.
Even where conservation attempts have been successful and
costs have been reduced there may well be positive opportunities to save money through the further tightening of
disciplines and through a well-timed reappraisal of energy
policies.

1. Ensure that energy conservation discipline is maintained ☐

Most companies appointed energy conservation committees
some years ago; a reconstituted team working on an energy
audit programme would make a valuable impact.

2. Maintain a high standard of 'housekeeping' ☐

Turning off lights, checking for air and steam leaks, shutting
doors and windows not only reduces waste but also engenders
a cost-conscious environment among the staff in relation to
energy costs.

3. Check meter accuracy □

Have them checked regularly.

4. Implement minor capital cost schemes to save energy □

Pipe lagging, window and door draught-proofing, double-glazing, wall insulation etc can save as much as 10 to 20 per cent of energy consumption.

5. Promote the theme of energy saving among your staff □

Everyone can help in this connection. Few people like to see waste of this nature; many would enjoy the opportunity of contributing to an energy saving campaign. Ask for ideas, run a competition, give prizes etc.

6. Make use of the films available from the Department of Energy □

A good film or video can often get the message across with more impact than verbal exhortations. They are available on free loan.

7. Keep in touch with the Local Regional Energy Efficiency Group □

Interchange of information at this high level of contact will stimulate ideas and action. Energy education is important, and regular revision will help.

8. Understand gas and electricity bills □

They can be quite complicated and tariffs should be studied carefully. Bills need to be checked and questioned where necessary. Energy suppliers' accounts should be scrutinised in depth and understood by those authorising payment.

9. Evaluate alternative tariff structures in order to obtain the most beneficial rate for your company □

By negotiating the tariff after such an evaluation a cheaper bill could result.

10. Be flexible with your factory and office central heating supervision □

Some companies switch their heating on or off according to a diary date, without regard to the temperature. This may result in windows being opened to let the heat out. A more flexible approach to the central heating annual 'switch on' may be advantageous.

11. Use independent advice □

Some energy consultants will review your energy policy and take a percentage of savings made for their fee. In this way you can't lose.

12. Install revolving doors □

Ordinary doors bring in up to ten times the amount of outside air as revolving doors.

13. Install warm air fans inside frequently used doors □

Now commonplace in stores and supermarkets, the practice is becoming more frequent in offices and factories.

14. Install time switches □

Time switches on lights, heating systems and fans can help to cut costs.

15. Change working hours according to climate □

By adjusting winter working hours (eg reducing the lunchtime break) you could close earlier, before the natural light fades and the temperature drops.

16. Convert waste materials or by-products into energy □

Take a good look at what you are throwing out as waste material and see if it could be recycled as energy.

17. Choose product designs and manufacturing methods with energy costs in mind □

Some products or piece parts may have been designed in the past specifying a method of manufacture with a high energy consumption factor. Take a good look at all your manu-facturing methods and processes which fall into this category and ask the design staff and their production methods col-leagues to come up with a more energy efficient design or process.

18. Make the most of the annual shut-down to modify existing plant and machinery to improve energy efficiency □

The plant manager could prepare a programme of work that could make the best use of this period.

19. Install larger capacity fuel storage tanks □

The price per unit of fuel may be less if the fuel order quantity is higher. Of course it will be necessary to justify the capital expenditure related to the potential saving.

20. Shut off the factory heating automatically when doors are open beyond a fixed period □

Imagine the heat loss when huge factory doors are opened for loading and unloading. Install a mechanism that shuts the factory heating off when doors are open beyond a certain time limit, otherwise you could be paying several times over each day for reheating the factory area.

21. Reduce heating and lighting levels either overall or in certain areas □

Heating and lighting areas where few personnel are employed or where there are no precious materials can be wasteful.

22. Coincide holidays with high energy consumption periods □

Additional days or weeks of holiday could be taken at times of the year when heating and lighting bills are high.

23. Keep maximum demand as low as possible □

A staggered machine start-up can keep the maximum electricity demand down.

24. Make use of cheaper electricity tariffs □

Use the cheaper tariffs wherever possible in your company premises.

25. Cost high energy cost operations into the selling price □

Certain products may absorb a high proportion of energy in their manufacturing process, justifying special costings and raised selling prices.

26. Control the use of internal transport □

Remember that internal transport such as fork lift trucks, conveyers etc uses up energy just like any other item of plant and machinery. Close supervision can reduce the movement of such vehicles and save energy.

27. Apply for grants □

The government and the EEC have operated a number of grant systems over the years in an attempt to encourage industry and commerce to save energy. The saving of energy obviously reduces costs for the user, so there is every reason to establish what schemes are currently available in this connection. Previous and current grant schemes are:

- Energy survey scheme
- Energy efficiency surveys
- Energy conservation demonstration projects scheme
- Support for innovation
- Industrial heat recovery scheme
- Coal firing scheme
- European Coal and Steel Community loans
- EEC energy efficiency assistance
- General government schemes covering energy efficiency.

28. Use tax incentives □

Make sure you are up-to-date with the current position regarding tax allowances affecting capital expenditure for the purpose of saving energy costs. The relevant legislation is reviewed each year.

29. Ask for free advice □

Consult any of the following for free advice:

- Regional energy efficiency officers
- Small Firms Centres (Department of Employment)
- Fuel suppliers
- Equipment suppliers
- Trade and research associations.

Chapter 15

Security

Crime in a variety of guises is on the increase. One of the major growth industries of our time is the supply of equipment to companies and individuals for deterring the thief. New devices for protecting vehicles and contractors' plant are now on the market to meet the rise in car and equipment theft. Your firm could be suffering a steady drain on its resources through petty or substantial theft. Save money by reviewing all aspects of security.

1. Regularly review your company security arrangements □

The thief soon spots any weaknesses in security routines that have been established and practised over a long period of time. These practices and routines become known to all concerned, including the thief, and the tendency is for slackness to creep into the routines anyway. A review of security practices will act as a deterrent.

2. Make the premises secure □

This may seem rather simple, but what may be adequate to the average executive or employee of the company may well be easy meat for the thief. Locks need to be changed from time to time and physical guarding of the premises and stocks should be thorough.

3. Use anti-theft devices on your company vehicles □

Three-quarters of a million vehicles are taken without the owner's consent every year in the UK. Many are gone for ever and those found are often damaged and occasionally beyond further use. The cost to the company lies in being unable to use that asset for some time. Vehicles can be taken from railway stations or airport car parks while you are away on business and can be shipped out of the country in next to no time. The same applies to contractors' plant on site location.

4. Siting of parking facilities for members of staff and visitors ☐

There are plenty of factories with limited parking arrangements which allow members of staff, visitors and even the public on occasion to park in close proximity to the factory or office buildings. This gives a first-class opportunity for the thief to carry out valuable items in his car boot.

5. Change the routines of your security officers ☐

Security officers and their routines should be altered regularly and without notice. Personnel should be made aware that you take this subject very seriously and that you are taking regular steps to reduce and eliminate offences. If you appear complacent, it will only encourage the problem.

6. Secure cash and valuables ☐

Many companies keep a strict procedure and control over petty cash but are not so strict over canteen tills, social club tills and other areas where there are cash and valuables lying around. Make a list of all points where cash is held and check that security is adequate.

7. Keep a record of office equipment ☐

Many items of office equipment are treated as a consumable expense rather than a capital expenditure. Therefore it is likely there is inadequate recording of their existence. This makes it very easy for dictating machines, calculators, typewriters etc to disappear without trace. A spot or regular inventory from time to time would help.

8. Control company petrol issued at the company pumps □

A free tankful of petrol is a temptation for anybody these days. An authorisation procedure coupled with physical spot checks at the pump and fuel consumption checks may well reveal that some individuals are using far more petrol than can be justified.

9. Keep a watch on consumable items in the factory □

A good number of consumable items such as tools, drills, yard brushes, oil, tape measures etc are an attractive proposition for personal use. In many instances there is little control over these items, so intermittent checks on consumption of the various types of consumable materials and tools, plus scrutiny of the main user departments, will improve security.

10. Limit the supply of protective and special clothing □

A number of companies supply special clothing such as jackets, overalls, gloves and shoes, all of which have a practical use outside the factory. It is also easy for special or protective clothing to be taken from a factory or office by simply wearing the outfit and walking out through the door.

11. Monitor scrap and reject materials properly □

This is a frequent and effective method for transferring high value items through the factory gate or office door. Each scrap or waste bin should be thoroughly inspected by a senior person for each department who should also insist that no item is put in the scrap or waste bin without his approval in the first place. A further check on the content of scrap bins should be made by the security staff at the gate and spot investigations should take place as necessary. Careful watch should be kept on the contents of scrap bins as they are weighed in on entering the factory premises. Scrap bins containing water show a high dead weight reading which can result in a lower tonnage of the contents being recorded when the skip is full and the water has been emptied.

12. Rely on stock records to pinpoint theft ☐

In the majority of cases companies allow some latitude in the accuracy of stock records compared with the physical count. Even perpetual inventory during the course of the year is still not sufficient to eliminate theft opportunity. Take a few items, preferably of high value, and take stock on a regular basis, perhaps once a day or even more frequently. This will allow you to pinpoint exactly the timing of theft and thereby identify the culprit. One tends to assume that discrepancies between the physical and stock records are due to some clerical error or miscount and in many companies it has become the accepted thing for such discrepancies to occur. Why not be suspicious for a time and consider that one or two discrepancies are the result of theft?

13. Guard against private work being carried out by individuals in the office or factory ☐

Company time spent on private or personal work in the office or factory is a costly matter. Again, it is quite normal for such things to happen but it can get out of hand, and when costs need to be kept to an absolute minimum it is a practice that many companies can ill afford. It is a subject worth bringing to the attention of managers both in the office and on the shop floor. Insist that such private work is eliminated.

14. Vet expense accounts ☐

This is a very easy way for individuals to obtain cash from the company. It requires only a little boldness on behalf of the claimant to put in the odd additional expense claim. Remember that vouchers are not difficult to come by.

15. Work the allotted hours ☐

There have been cases of employees clocking on and clocking off but disappearing in between.

16. Control abuse of the firm's post room □

Private mail can sometimes creep in, so keep an eye open for this. Even just a few letters a day (especially if they're for overseas) can add up to a heavy bill over a year.

17. Keep a proper record of goods on loan or on demonstration □

Once goods have left the premises they should be invoiced, even if on an 'on loan' basis. All stocks not under your physical control should be accounted for by the finance department and a report of such goods which have been given out on loan for exhibitions and shows or for demonstration purposes should be regularly studied.

18. Authorise all credit notes □

The issuing of credit notes on the request of a junior person without proper authorisation by a senior or independent person is a bad practice. All credit notes should be independently assessed, audited and authorised.

19. Check that all goods despatched and services rendered by the company are invoiced □

As with credit notes, the non-invoicing of goods despatched or services rendered by a company is an opportunity for theft by conspiring persons. It is also a very expensive loss to the company. A regular calculation by the finance department should reconcile opening and closing order values by adjusting for orders received and invoices raised in the period.

20. Allocate cash received to the relevant sales ledger account □

Some companies have suffered as a result of incoming cheques and cash being incorrectly allocated to customer accounts, thus enabling the person involved to redirect cash easily. This practice can go undetected for years unless steps are taken to check on it.

21. Check payroll calculations □

Many companies operate bonus schemes which can be man-ipulated. Payment by results often reduces unit cost but it is essential that the results are measured accurately. Incorrect recording of batch quantities can result in higher wages and a higher unit cost.

22. Check incoming materials □

Over-booking of incoming materials can lead to over-payments and shortages on production. Both are unaccept-ably costly for your company. Make sure that the weighbridge at the goods reception point is accurate and that calculated weights and quantities come acceptably close to invoiced quantities.

23. Investigate despatch shortages □

Goods can disappear from company or hauliers' vehicles and this usually results in a claim for a shortage from the client. Make sure that goods are despatched accurately and are properly protected against theft during transit.

24. Insist that shortages are claimed within a very short time □

Claims for delivery shortages should be made very soon, or be invalidated. Once the goods have left your premises you become vulnerable to outside influences. Goods could be stolen *en route* or at your client's premises. Therefore it is essential that goods delivered by you are checked by the recipient immediately on receipt and shortages notified to you there and then. Claims for shortages within a period in excess of a few days should be resisted.

25. Practise fire drill regularly □

Fire drills can often turn out to be a shambles and sometimes even comic. Check that your fire prevention officers are still aware of their duties and that all employees are trained in what to do in the event of a fire alarm. Have a fire drill without notice and see what reaction you get. Then count the cost of such a response in a real emergency.

26. Make use of the free survey offered by the fire brigade ☐

Firms specialising in the provision of fire fighting equipment and its maintenance will carry out a survey for you. The outcome may be that you are advised to replace old or obsolete equipment. That costs money, so make use of the fire brigade for a free independent survey of your fire prevention equipment and procedures.

27. Have an effective Health and Safety Committee ☐

Make the best possible use of your Health and Safety Committee. Don't let it become a complaints department. Steer its activities sensibly so that protection of your company and your employees can be improved.

28. Insure adequately ☐

The effect on your company of the theft of a vital piece of equipment or of a major tragedy such as a fire or explosion could be catastrophic and terminal. (See pages 85–6.)

29. Be advised of material interests ☐

An employee having a 'material interest' in a contract could be in a position to influence matters to his advantage rather than to the company's.

Chapter 16

Insurance

1. Insure adequately □

The scope of your insurance cover is a matter of judgement which will be influenced by the insurance broker and the insurance companies. However, too much influence may result in over-caution and a higher premium cost than necessary. A well-balanced view of the degree of risk you to take is essential.

2. Review your cover independently □

This will help with your assessment and may prevent your drifting into too much or too little insurance.

3. Insure against major catastrophes □

A single major disaster could ruin your business. So fire insurance and the like must be properly organised. You may be able to absorb minor losses but not big ones.

4. Self-insurance □

Occasions may arise when the premium paid is greater than the likely maximum loss or inconvenience to your business. Self-insurance may be justified in such circumstances, and when you take a 'view' of the risk the premium savings may be quite high. Remember to set aside adequate provision.

5. Obtain competitive quotes □

If you have tended to stick with the familiar you may all too readily accept the premiums levied on you. Start investigating next year's insurance requirements well before the renewal date.

6. Make long-term arrangements ☐

If you choose to make a longer-term commitment to a selected firm you may obtain premium benefits.

7. Group insurance policies ☐

Combined policies may be cheaper. Your trade or professional association may be able to offer an insurance 'package' which covers many of your needs.

8. Take action to reduce the premiums ☐

The higher the risk, the higher the premium – so reduce the risk where you can. Most insurance companies will advise you on particularly hazardous practices and by taking those extra precautions, savings are available.

9. Accept an excess in your policies ☐

By paying the first minor part of the claim, premiums can be reduced.

Chapter 17

Slow Moving and Obsolete Stock

Most manufacturing and commercial concerns that hold trading stock find themselves having to write off a certain proportion of their stock value at the end of each financial year in respect of slow moving and obsolete stock. The strange thing is that, although the goods and materials were probably purchased by profit-responsible executives of the comapany, it is usually the financial staff who determine what and how much should be written off each year.

Accountants usually make provision in their accounts for stock which everyone agrees is definitely obsolete and unsaleable in the normal course of business. They also determine the write-off in respect of obsolete and slow moving stock on the basis of the age of the stock or perhaps a percentage of the stock value. Such arithmetically conceived write-offs are in accordance with accounting standards and conventions which require that accounts are drawn up on a reasonably prudent basis. Very often the detail of these various provisions is invisible to other members of the company. Perhaps greater visibility would help your company to establish sensible policies with regards to using or liquidating such stocks.

1. Schedule all obsolete and slow moving stock □

With a detailed analysis of such stock, accompanied by an explanation as to just why each item of stock has been classified obsolete or slow moving, the whole management of the company can take executive action to ensure that they are not repeating the same mistakes. If policies and practices continue unchanged, there is some likelihood of increasing the cost of obsolete and slow moving stock each year, whereas you should be taking action to decrease it.

2. Physically separate obsolete stock from current stock □

In many companies obsolete stock is only summarised by a schedule annexed to the year-end accounts. In this way only the accounts staff are aware of its existence. In practice, because few people know the details of the stock, and because it is spread around the factory and warehouse, it will tend to remain there year after year without anybody being aware of its stock value classification. If it is physically separated it means far more to every employee than would a list prepared by the accounts department. Obsolete stock has to be tackled as a separate problem and its physical separation from the rest of the stock-in-trade of the company will assist the identification of disposal opportunities.

3. Nominate executive responsibility □

Disposal of existing obsolete stock and avoidance of building up new obsolete stock can often be a major task, requiring the full-time effort of an experienced all-rounder in the company.

4. Make factory management aware of the stock □

Factory management means not only the works director and manager but everyone down the line from the foreman and charge hands to the administrative staff in production control and planning etc. By modifying slow moving or apparently obsolete stock it may be possible for the manufacturing divisions to bring the stocks into line with present-day designs, thus avoiding duplicated production costs.

5. Make the design department aware of the stock □

Again, the design department can play a part in solving the problem. By modifying a proposed design for a new product or part, it is possible that existing stocks, particularly of raw materials and components, can be used.

6. Make the purchasing department aware of the stock □

The purchasing department could play a part by ensuring that no purchase requisition is converted into an order before they are satisfied that current slow moving and obsolete stock cannot be used.

7. Accept the reality of obsolete stock ☐

It is sometimes very difficult for management to bring itself to accept the reality of the situation. It is often easier and more convenient to bury the problem and hope that it will go away in time. Rather, accept the reality of the situation and do what you can to liquidate the stocks so that you are no longer paying a stock holding cost in the form of rent, rates, bank interest etc. Try to avoid cluttering your warehouse and branches with stocks which there is no reasonable chance of liquidating without lowering prices and making a special effort.

8. Sell stock back to the supplier ☐

The proprietary article that you may be classifying as obsolete may be so classified simply because your own end product has changed. This does not mean to say that the article could not be used elsewhere. Perhaps the most sensible way for you to de-stock would be for your buying department to arrange for the articles concerned to be returned to the supplier. The supplier may be reluctant to give full credit, but even if you only get a proportion of the cost price by returning them, you will still probably receive more this way than you would by trying to sell the items on the open market. Many suppliers are willing to do this as it is a means for them to make profit and at the same time fosters goodwill.

9. Try auctioning obsolete stock ☐

This is often the fastest way of getting rid of those unwanted stocks, the advantage being that you know your selling costs in advance as they are usually calculated as a percentage of the proceeds. Cash receipt is immediate.

10. Avoid obsolete stock □

One of the most frequent causes of obsolete stock is the introduction of a new product, launched with a flurry of enthusiasm by the marketing department but without regard to
the fact that slow moving and obsolete stock has been
created.

11. Be realistic about stock values generally □

The inflation of recent years has tended to increase stock
values. Taxation concessions have also encouraged increases.
In reality, however, the net realisable value of stock may be
decreasing as world markets shrink. Stock valued at today's
inflated cost levels may ultimately only be saleable at a lower
market price.

12. Arrange joint buying arrangements □

By joining forces with other users of similar materials and
components, your joint requirements may equal the
minimum production batch size that the suppliers are willing
to produce. In this way you will avoid obsolete stock resulting
from enforced over-purchasing.

Chapter 18

New Products and Product Improvements

Managers enjoy being involved in success and so will be full of enthusiasm as sales of a new product start to take off. Expansion and sales development from an increased range of products or a wider geographical area will not find enthusiasm or hard work wanting.

But how do we foresee the end of a product's lifespan? Be prepared for it with a policy for new products and product improvements.

1. Prepare a product improvement plan □

If your present products are selling well you cannot be blamed for feeling satisfied. However, your competitors are watching you with envy and will not have been idle. They are probably working at this very moment on a product with a few advantageous features, so don't ever think that your current product design is the ultimate. There will be changes in style, custom, fashion, new technology etc. Ensure that your programme of product improvement keeps you ahead.

2. Be wary of demands for changes in product design □

How often do you have sales conferences at which there are complaints about product design, such as its colour, size or capacity? These can be excuses for poor sales, and not genuinely constructive ideas for product improvement.

3. Market product improvements correctly □

When you see the TV adverts for consumer products, you have to marvel at how a minor product change is launched to the public; it is so successful that sales increase. The improvement may be very slight, but nevertheless those professionals seem able to take advantage of every single product improvement as an opportunity to put over yet again all the features and benefits of their particular product.

4. Provide incentives for product search □

Few of us are capable of thinking of something that is absolutely brand-new. However, that doesn't mean to say that there isn't someone in your organisation who may perhaps inadvertently come up with a good idea. So provide an incentive. Have a competition for your employees and give prizes to those who produce good ideas for new products and product improvements. Give double prizes for those who come up with new products that can be made from existing standard components and piece-parts.

5. Ask the market for advice on new products □

Don't forget it's the market place that determines demand. Encourage ideas from customers and your own sales staff who are regularly in touch with the market place. Sometimes we can be guilty of thinking that ideas from customers and sales staff are really criticisms, but listen carefully and you will learn what the market really wants. Customers often come up with the best ideas.

6. Pay attention to installation and service engineers □

The people who really know how good your product is in practice are your installers and service engineers, and your dealers and outlets that have to make the product work. They can often make recommendations which are more readily listened to, as they are not putting over a sales pitch.

7. Obtain the commitment of dealers and sales staff □

Enthusiasm for a new product can often wane just as the product is about to be launched. This is because an idea is now becoming a reality and those who were in favour of a particular product development are now faced with the task of having to turn that enthusiasm into hard-earned orders. For any new product to be successfully launched, it is of the utmost importance to get the complete commitment of your sales staff, dealers, customers etc before you incur any expenditure.

8. Avoid being misled into believing that a market exists □

How many times have you heard people say, 'There is an enormous market for it', or 'the market potential must be huge'? A market exists only where there is money available which can willingly be exchanged for your goods. Don't be misled into believing that a market exists just because somebody else is enjoying high-volume sales of a particular product.

9. Monitor expenditure on new products □

It is easy to incur unnecessary expenditure in research and development. Product development must not be the whim of any one person. It must be based on sound commercial strategy and the financial department should be closely involved in drawing up a detailed budget to be agreed both by those incurring the expenditure in product development and those who will be responsible for recovering that expendiure in future sales.

10. Keep up-to-date with what is going on in the world □

A number of managers, especially those who have been in the same company or trade for most of their lives, tend to feel they know it all. They are guilty of taking a limited or restrictive view of business developments. Perhaps they are too set in their ways. Analyse yourself and your staff and see whether or not you need to take a step outside your present environment for a short while, just to make sure that you are really up-to-date with modern market needs and new technology. Then you can return to the task of making sure that your company's products are the best, most modern and will bring really good returns for your business.

11. Test the product thoroughly prior to launch ☐

Your new product won't get off the ground unless you test it *before* the launch. Customers hate being guinea pigs and will start looking elsewhere for supplies, as well as returning faulty goods for recompense.

12. Plan the termination of a product's lifespan ☐

If a new product is intended to replace an existing one, it is essential to time the introduction of the new product so as to allow stocks of the existing product to be sold first. Be careful not to 'land' stocks of old models on a valued customer's lap, as he will resent being overstocked and be unable to take up stocks of the new model. Try to find a market that will willingly accept the old models so that all your valued customers can be involved to the full in the new product launch.

13. Design for the total market ☐

So often companies take the view that a new product should be designed to suit its national market. Following a successful home market launch, export markets are then sought, only to find that the designers have omitted to consider international trends, fashions, standards etc. By adopting this approach you have said farewell to your biggest market.

14. Keep designers in line ☐

Some design work never ends. As soon as one bit of design work is completed someone comes up with an idea to improve upon it. These good ideas grow in momentum to the point where the designers are seeking the ideal rather than the practicable. At some stage new product development has to leave the drawing board and appear on the price list.

15. Ensure designers are aware of product costs ☐

Products should be designed to be manufactured at a pre-determined cost. Unless the designers are aware of the cost impact of their work, they will exceed the product cost budget. Feed them with alternative material and production costs so that there is no disappointment at the end.

16. Set target dates for the completion of new product designs ☐

If no target dates are agreed, months or possibly years of valuable sales time will be lost. Set target dates and review them regularly. Don't allow excuses for delay.

17. Keep an eye on your competitors ☐

Keep track on your competitors' activities but at the same time plug the leaks in your own organisation. Limit the number of people with whom your secrets are shared. Premature disclosure prevents patent registration.

18. Be involved in the appropriate trade associations etc ☐

Trade associations can often give you the necessary leads for investigating growth areas. Keep in touch with them and also the appropriate government departments, aid programmes and the relevant pressure groups.

19. Use university and college facilities ☐

Academic establishments possess excellent specialist skills both in their members of staff and students. They can be approached to give you the benefit of their academic knowledge, although it will be up to you to turn it into something of practical use. In addition, both universities and colleges have laboratory equipment which you may be able to use.

20. Obtain government grants □

Make sure you have researched all grant opportunities. Grants are there to be used, so use them when you can.

Chapter 19

Pricing Policy

Companies can increase profit either by cost reduction or by margin improvements. Margin improvement or improvement in the gross profit can be achieved either by increasing unit selling prices or by increasing sales volume (this includes the possibility of reducing unit selling prices in order to be more competitive and increase sales volume).

Selling prices are affected by supply, demand and cost conditions. All companies need to ensure that their pricing policy gives the best opportunity for maximising sales and profits.

1. Keep pace with inflation ☐

The inflation rate is the percentage rate per period that prices are increasing and should provide a guideline to the level of price increases generally.

2. Keep an eye on competitors' price movements ☐

In a falling market businesses tend to take a more flexible approach to pricing in order to obtain a larger share of a diminishing market. In these circumstances a rigid and inflexible approach to pricing allows your competitors to take a proportion of your business. Smaller companies – which are growing in number day by day – with lower overheads are able to react very quickly and obtain orders through price flexibility. It is essential, therefore, that you know what your competitors are doing and that you adapt to the challenge of the circumstances.

3. Maintain information regarding changing price levels in the market place □

A business will only survive if it continues to receive orders from clients. It will only receive orders from clients as long as it is competitive. It is therefore necessary to ensure that policy decisions take account of the severity of price competition in the market place. Arrange to receive lost order reports from your sales staff, dealers etc. These reports should concentrate on orders lost on price.

4. Adjust selling prices to compensate for previous across the board increases □

As an expedient, price increases are often fixed on an across the board percentage basis per product group. This may have resulted in distortions which need to be corrected. Some prices may be a few points too high or too low, thus affecting your margin or competitiveness.

5. Take advantage of market sectors in which you have a monopoly □

Unlike the normal laws of economics, price changes do not affect demand to the same extent where you have a monopoly. Prices for some of your products for which there is little or no competition, for example spares and service, can enjoy a higher mark-up.

6. Identify the price leader in your industry □

Some industries are dominated by a few sellers who set the trend for selling prices. Certain companies emerge as price leaders and others in the industry set their prices accordingly. Therefore it is important to assess correctly your relationship with your industry price leader. You may well be the price leader yourself, or it may be a competitor, either larger or smaller than you. Determine how your industry reacts to a change in prices by one of its members and identify the reaction of others in the industry – do they change their prices? Also identify the reaction of the customers – do they re-source their requirements? Some firms will always be a small percentage cheaper than the leaders no matter what their price level, and others will always be slightly higher. Their pricing strategy may be determined on the basis that they can survive adequately by taking that share of the market available to them at a slightly lower or a slightly higher price.

7. Recognise the effects of windfall profits on your selling price policy □

Profits (or lack of them) are usually reflected in the selling price policy. Low profits or losses can encourage price increases and high profits can encourage stability. Windfall profits or short-run profits should be adjusted for when determining your pricing policy. A large single order may have earned an adequate sales margin or provided full activity in the factory for a period. Such benefit may not be enjoyed in the future, however, so selling price policy should take windfall profits into account and therefore base the strategy on the underlying and continuing activities of the business.

8. Calculate the effect on profits of reduction in price □

Salesmen like to reduce prices in order to encourage sales, but the effect of doing so has always to be considered most carefully. Always calculate by how much sales must increase to achieve the same result as before. The effect of a price reduction is always to reduce the profit volume ratio and to raise the break-even point and shorten the margin of safety. When reducing prices to earn more business, ensure that there is a commitment to increase sales which results in an increased margin for the company.

9. Strategic divisionalising of the policy □

Your pricing policies are first and foremost intended to result in a profit for your company. There are several instances where an adjustment in price can achieve a particular objective, such as:

- the maintenance of present activity levels;
- to dispose of slow moving stock;
- to introduce a new product to the market;
- to deter the competition;
- to increase the sales of other products by the use of loss leaders.

You should always proceed with utmost caution and remember that the main objective is to achieve a profit for each and every item you sell.

10. Evaluate the cost of price reduction in the form of discounts □

If discounts are part of your pricing policy they need to be evaluated in just the same way as any other expenditure. Without a corresponding increase in sales a price reduction simply takes a slice of the profits or adds to the losses.

11. Review the discount policy □

Again, this needs to be positively reviewed periodically. Discount review may provide an opportunity for increasing your company profits. A change of emphasis may change product sales mix to your advantage.

12. Educate the sales and commercial staff about the purpose of the discount policy □

In many companies pricing policy is determined at management level and then issued as a policy to the sales team. Perhaps if they were aware of the reasoning behind the policy, the objectives might be achieved more quickly.

13. Examine discounts/price reductions □

There may be a tendency for certain sales areas, product or customer groups to be rather more costly than the average. Certain sales staff may offer discounts as their main plank to achieve a sale whereas another sales person taking a different tack may be just as successful without incurring the same cost. Similarly, customer or product groups need to be watched, and branches and divisions also.

14. Control discounts □

Referrals to management for approval to allow a discount enable the manager to have control of the cost of discounts.

15. Link discounts to a specific benefit for your company □

Wherever possible, discounts should be earned by the customer. Discounts may be more cost-effective for your company if they are linked to customer performance levels, eg bulk orders, prompt payment, target achievement, stock levels, market support etc. At the very least, try to make the customer feel as though he has to earn his discount. Otherwise he may look upon you as an easy touch and you will end up selling discounts instead of products.

16. Relate discounts on sales to discounts on purchases □

It is a good sign if your buying is as profitable as your selling. As a general guide you should be earning discounts on purchases equal to, or at least in proportion to, the discounts you are giving to your customers.

17. Examine the effect of an increase in selling price on profitability □

In the same way as companies frequently calculate the effect on profits of a reduction in selling prices, a calculation of the effects of the opposite alternative may be worthwhile. Such an upward movement in price levels may result in a downward demand. A lower level of profits may not necessarily follow and for certain loss-making product groups it doesn't follow that losses will increase. A lower activity level at better prices could be more profitable. Such a policy will give you the opportunity of examining all other operating cost levels.

18. Calculate break-even points and profit volume ratios per product group or division ☐

The finance department can calculate the optimum mix/ volume of your products sales to achieve the highest overall level of profitability.

19. Use the occasion of a price increase as an opportunity to increase sales ☐

Try and roll a price increase into as attractive a package as possible for your customers. By giving advance warning of the effective date of an increase and by timing the increase to coincide with a slack period in the year you can capture additional sales. Be careful, however, to avoid simply bringing forward orders that you would have received anyway and at a better price. At all times make sure that out-of-season discounts are of real benefit to you.

20. Present your prices in the most suitable manner for your customers ☐

Orders can be lost because the pricing policy falls short of what the client really needs. Every customer wants to know how much the product is going to cost him. That is inclusive of such items as packing, delivery, installation, insurance, freight etc. A client in an overseas market is unlikely to be impressed with an ex works unpacked price. He needs to know the total cost or at least have to hand enough information, such as a packing specification, to enable him to calculate the total.

21. Offer prices in the right currency ☐

Only rarely would you willingly buy a product priced in a currency other than that of the country in which your business is situated. Similarly, clients will look favourably at prices in their own currency. Selling in foreign currencies is a specialised business but most banks employ specialists who are available to help.

22. Make sure that price lists are clear to the reader □

An unclear price list can lose business so easily. Unless it is legible and intelligible, many customers lose interest immediately. Don't confuse the price list with too many technical facts or options.

23. Investigate alternative channels of distribution □

With the modern methods of communication, customer contact is easier and quicker. This may enable you to simplify your channels of distribution and improve your competitiveness. Your pricing policy would obviously come under review.

24. Use all available channels of distribution □

It is possible to use several channels of distribution to dispose of your goods and services to your best advantage. Don't let your present customary distribution channels restrict your sales and profit levels. Double check that your prices are not uplifted to pay for superfluous middlemen, resulting in lack of competitiveness or low profits. Alternatively, a middleman may be able to carry out the function more cheaply than you can. By spreading his selling costs over a wide range of products a wholesaler may be able to sell a product at a lower price than the manufacturer could.

25. Obtain a satisfactory return on quotations □

When preparing an estimate for a quotation, companies should ensure that the most competitive price has been offered. Estimates are bound by price build-up formulae determined by the finance department and based on future cost levels. But has a really competitive approach been made at the quotation stage? Commitment should be sought from the design, manufacturing, transport and other departments. If you're looking for orders get constructive help from everyone you can.

26. Be careful not to undersell your products and services ☐

The ability to sell at a high price depends on the relative strengths and weaknesses of the seller and buyer. It is quite easy to persuade yourself that for one reason or another your position is relatively weaker than the buyer's, so you try to compensate for this by selling at a lower price. As you can rarely have a 'take it or leave it' approach when selling, it is important to ensure that sales staff have full confidence in the company and its products. Time and effort should be given towards building up that confidence and optimism which, once gained, will result in higher sales and better prices.

27. Base selling prices on actual product costs ☐

Selling prices should be related to actual costs, with a mark-up for profit. The costing system must therefore provide cost information in a manner directly comparable with your pricing policy. Otherwise, you're in the dark.

28. Ensure through the pricing policy formula that total revenue will exceed total costs by an acceptable margin ☐

Direct costs should be correctly collated – usually not too difficult an exercise. But the total of the mark-up per product multiplied by the number of units to be sold must finally recover all non-direct costs and give a sensible and worthwhile reward for your efforts in the form of profits.

29. Charge extra costs ☐

Make sure that, where there are changes in the order specification after the order has been accepted, proper records are maintained to enable you to charge for extras.

Chapter 20

Carriage Costs

It is tempting for companies to pay less time and attention than they should to the cost of carriage. It is sometimes felt that once the goods have left the plant the job has been completed, and the carriage is left to outside hauliers or your own firm's transport. Carriage can, however, be a useful profit centre and if properly managed can provide a worthwhile contribution to your operating performance.

1. Recover carriage outwards charges □

Each despatch should show a profit on the outward carriage and checks should be made to relate hauliers' invoices to outward charges.

2. Recover carriage inwards costs □

Carriage inwards for all your supplies, both direct and indirect, should be costed into your product costs to ensure that carriage inwards is not an unrecovered overhead.

3. Pass your carriage purchases through the disciplines of the buying office □

It is quite easy for carriage arrangements to be made by a despatch department in a hurry to meet delivery dates. This can sometimes mean that these last-minute arrangements bypass your rigorous purchasing routines.

4. Receive competitive quotes from a selection of reliable hauliers □

There can be a tendency to keep with the same haulier simply because the driver carries out a regular periodical run to a given area and this becomes a routine. Despite the reliability of such a routine it is advisable to obtain frequent checks on prices.

5. Check the accuracy of transport volumes ☐

With some products a transport volume is calculated according to the method of packing and this is the basis of the haulier's charge, dependent on the distance taken. As manufacturing and packing methods change you should ensure that your transport volumes are recalculated.

6. Schedule despatches properly ☐

Avoid repeat journeys by collating deliveries to the same area.

7. Control 'special' deliveries ☐

With the advent of many excellent overnight services it is easy for such services to become the norm rather than special. Although they are reliable and speedy, don't forget that they cost extra and somebody has to foot the bill. Either ensure that the charge is passed on or that regular transport is used except in emergencies.

Chapter 21

Packing and Freight

Exporting companies need cost-effective packing and packaging in order to be competitive in world markets. Freight costs are based on volumes or weights and manufacturers can pay unnecessarily for thin air because of ineffective packaging.

1. Design products with freight costs in mind □

Where possible product design should result in the smallest and lightest package to reduce freight costs. This can include products for local part assembly or completely knocked down. Local assembly costs can be less than freight costs and have the added attraction of providing some local participation.

2. Make sure crates and cases are as cheap as they can be □

Companies who have traditionally exported for many years should look at the materials used and the design of their packaging. Look at the use of crates as opposed to cases and also consider the use of cartons as an alternative.

3. Make maximum use of container transport □

Containerised transport requires less packaging.

4. Use your freight company to the best advantage □

With containerisation, roll on/roll off transport etc, new opportunities arise for cheaper freight. Always pressurise your freight agent to find the cheapest route.

5. Obtain discount for freight quantity □

Negotiate with your shipping agent a discount based on the value of business you give him. Commit yourself to this value and obtain the discount which will be a useful contribution to your profits.

6. Consider purchasing second-hand containers □

Cheaper rates can be obtained if you purchase second-hand containers and leave them on site. This may have the added advantage of providing a site storage facility during the course of a construction.

Chapter 22

Company Transport

Some companies find operating their own transport division to be more profitable than using outside hauliers. Others maintain a small vehicle division as a convenience.

1. Be aware of comparative vehicle operating costs □

When purchasing a new vehicle always compare the running cost per mile of the various vehicles available. The purchase price of vehicles can mislead you into buying the cheapest but you need to consider the whole cost, both capital and operating costs during the vehicle's life.

2. Advertise for cargo to fill up a vehicle □

Other local manufacturers may be willing to use your transport for their own goods which will be very helpful, especially when you only have part loads.

3. Obtain return loads □

An empty vehicle really is a waste and an effort should be made to obtain a return load. Perhaps you could bring in supplies which are subject to an addition for carriage, thus eliminating the carriage cost.

4. Use petrol facilities at other companies/branches within your group □

The facility to use fuel from other group sites would add to the benefit of purchasing petrol in bulk.

Further Reading from Kogan Page

Be Your Own Company Secretary, A J Scrine, 1987

Be Your Own PR Man, 2nd edition, Michael Bland, 1987

Business Rip-Offs and How to Avoid Them, Tony Attwood, 1987

Buying for Business: How to Get the Best Deal from Your Suppliers, Tony Attwood, 1988

Choosing and Using Professional Advisers, ed Paul Chaplin, 1986

Customer Service, Malcolm Peel, 1987

Debt Collection Made Easy, Peter Buckland, 1987

Do Your Own Market Research, Paul N Hague and Peter Jackson, 1987

Expenses and Benefits of Directors and Higher Paid Employees, John F Staddon, annual

Financial Management for the Small Business: a Daily Telegraph Guide, 2nd edition, Colin Barrow, 1988

The First-Time Manager, M J Morris, 1988

How to Make Meetings Work, Malcolm Peel, 1988

Make Every Minute Count, Marion E Haynes, 1988

Profits from Improved Productivity, Fiona Halse and John Humphrey, 1988

How to Organise Effective Conferences and Meetings, David Seekings, 3rd edition, 1987

The Practice of Successful Business Management, Kenneth Winckles, 1986